LP
11/12

THE BLUE SHARK

By Sara Green

BELLWETHER MEDIA • MINNEAPOLIS, MN

Jump into the cockpit and take flight with Pilot books. Your journey will take you on high-energy adventures as you learn about all that is wild, weird, fascinating, and fun!

This edition first published in 2013 by Bellwether Media, Inc.

No part of this publication may be reproduced in whole or in part without written permission of the publisher. For information regarding permission, write to Bellwether Media, Inc., Attention: Permissions Department, 5357 Penn Avenue South, Minneapolis, MN 55419.

Library of Congress Cataloging-in-Publication Data

Green, Sara, 1964-
The blue shark / by Sara Green.
    p. cm. – (Pilot books: shark fact files)
Includes bibliographical references and index.
Summary: "Engaging images accompany information about the blue shark. The combination of high-interest subject matter and narrative text is intended for students in grades 3 through 7"–Provided by publisher.
ISBN 978-1-60014-802-6 (hardcover : alk. paper)
  1. Blue shark–Juvenile literature. I. Title.
QL638.95.C3G74 2013
597.3'4–dc23

                    2012000450

Printed in the United States of America, North Mankato, MN.

TABLE OF CONTENTS

BLUE SHARK
IDENTIFIED

Two divers swim into a metal cage in the ocean. The cage keeps them safe, but the divers are still nervous. This is shark territory! Soon, a large fish with long, pointed **pectoral fins** swims toward them. The divers recognize its dark blue back, bright blue sides, and white underbelly. It is a blue shark, one of the fastest predators in the ocean.

The shark is hungry and curious. It bumps its snout against the cage. Suddenly, **nictitating membranes** close over its round, black eyes. This signals an attack! The shark's razor-sharp teeth clamp down on the bars of the cage. The shark soon loses interest and swims away in search of tastier prey. The divers are relieved and thrilled at the same time. It is rare to be so close to a dangerous predator!

5

The blue shark is found in the Pacific, Atlantic, and Indian Oceans. This shark prefers to cruise the open ocean, but it will sometimes come near shore. It can swim to depths of 1,150 feet (350 meters).

The blue shark's coloring has an important purpose. Seen from below, the shark blends in with the sunlit surface. Seen from above, it gets lost in the darker water beneath it. This countershading allows it to sneak up on prey. It also helps the shark stay hidden from predators.

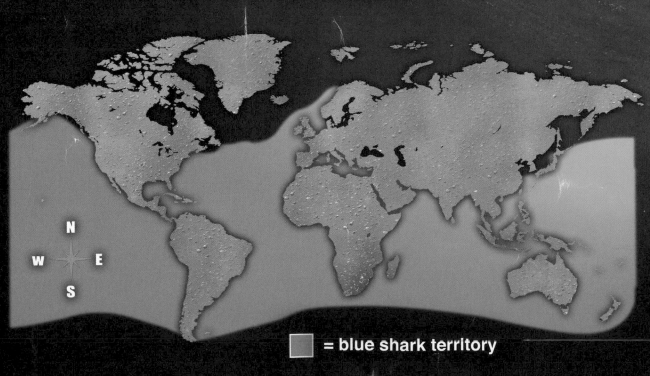

= blue shark territory

human

blue shark

The blue shark is not a large shark. Most adults are
6 to 8 feet (1.8 to 2.4 meters) long and weigh between
65 and 115 pounds (30 and 52 kilograms). However,
some can reach a length of 12 feet (3.6 meters) and
weigh up to 500 pounds (225 kilograms)!

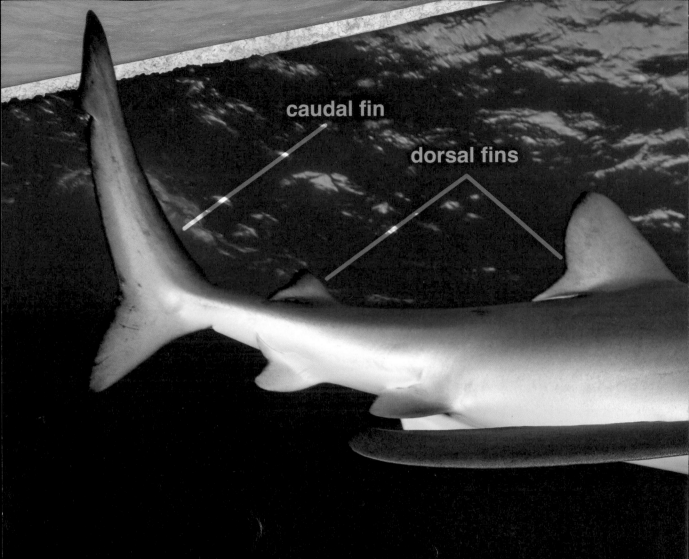

caudal fin

dorsal fins

The blue shark's body is built for speed. Many
researchers say its top speed is around 22 miles
(35 kilometers) per hour, but some believe it can swim as
fast as 60 miles (97 kilometers) per hour! The blue shark
has two **dorsal fins**. They help the shark balance.
The tail fin is called the **caudal fin**. The blue shark
sweeps it from side to side to gain power and speed.

A female blue shark's skin is three times thicker than a male's skin. This protects females from the bites of males when they mate.

The blue shark's skin is covered with a layer of small, overlapping scales called dermal denticles. These protect the shark and help it move smoothly through water. A shark's skeleton is made of cartilage. This lets the blue shark swim, bend, and turn quickly in the water.

BLUE SHARK TRACKED

Female blue sharks are viviparous. The shark pups develop inside the mother. After 9 to 12 months, the mother gives birth to a litter of live young. Most litters contain 25 to 50 pups. Some have as few as 4 or as many as 135! Larger mothers tend to have larger litters. At birth, each pup is 16 to 20 inches (40 to 51 centimeters) long. Pups are born with teeth. They are ready to hunt and survive on their own.

Sharks mature slower than most other fish. Blue sharks become adults between the ages of 4 and 6. Many scientists believe blue sharks live 20 years or longer.

young blue shark

Every year, most blue sharks **migrate** long distances. Scientists use special equipment to track blue sharks as they travel. Small electronic tags are attached to the dorsal fins of the sharks. These tags measure the depth and temperature of each shark's surroundings. In time, the tags detach and float to the surface. They send information to computers for the scientists to study.

Researchers have learned that blue sharks travel to warm waters in the fall and winter. They return to cool waters in the spring and summer.

A LONG JOURNEY

The longest recorded migration for a tagged blue shark was 3,740 miles (6,020 kilometers). It traveled south in the Atlantic Ocean from New York to Brazil.

THE HUNTER BECOMES THE HUNTED

Blue sharks can also be prey for larger animals. Great white sharks, mako sharks, and California sea lions hunt and eat blue sharks.

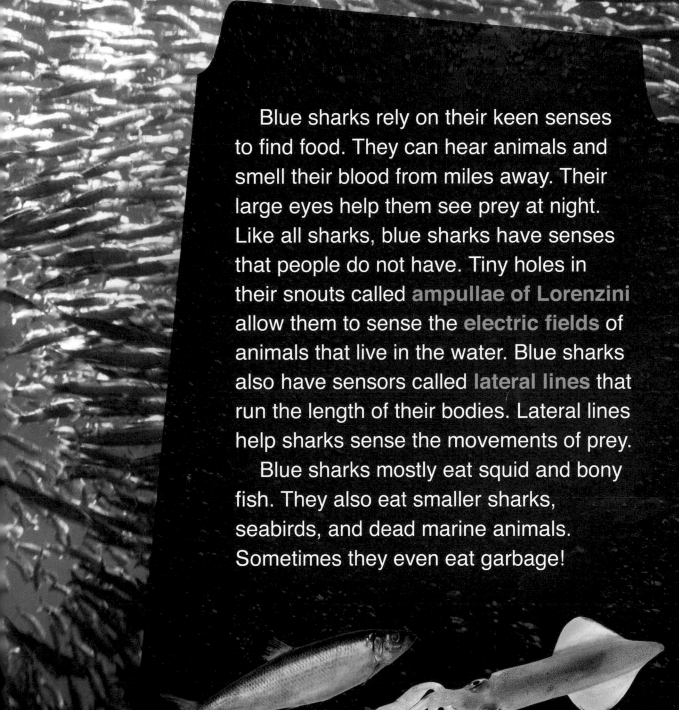

Blue sharks rely on their keen senses to find food. They can hear animals and smell their blood from miles away. Their large eyes help them see prey at night. Like all sharks, blue sharks have senses that people do not have. Tiny holes in their snouts called ampullae of Lorenzini allow them to sense the electric fields of animals that live in the water. Blue sharks also have sensors called lateral lines that run the length of their bodies. Lateral lines help sharks sense the movements of prey.

Blue sharks mostly eat squid and bony fish. They also eat smaller sharks, seabirds, and dead marine animals. Sometimes they even eat garbage!

bony fish

squid

The blue shark has several rows of long, **serrated** teeth. The first two rows help capture, hold, and rip apart prey. When these teeth are lost or broken, teeth from the back rows move forward to take their place. Upper teeth curve inward and their bases overlap. Lower teeth are straight and narrow. This arrangement helps the blue shark hang on to slippery prey.

The blue shark will sometimes swim with its mouth wide open to catch tiny animals such as anchovies and krill. Unlike most other predatory sharks, the blue shark has **gill rakers** that catch these tiny creatures.

BLUE SHARK
CURRENT STATUS

Many scientists worry about the future of the blue shark. Every year, between 10 and 20 million blue sharks are killed. Their fins are used to make shark fin soup. The cartilage is used for medicine, and the skin is made into leather. People enjoy catching the blue shark for sport. Many blue sharks also end up as **bycatch** in fishing nets and on long fishing lines meant for other fish. The blue shark is listed as **near threatened** by the International Union for Conservation of Nature (IUCN).

No laws stop people from catching the blue shark. However, many scientists encourage fishers to limit how many they catch. They teach people that the blue shark is not a fearsome monster. It is a predator that has an important place in the ocean **ecosystem**. It keeps prey populations from growing too large.

SHARK BRIEF

Common Name: Blue Shark

Nickname: Wolf of the Sea

Claim to Fame: Longest migration

Hot Spots: Caribbean
New England
Iberian Peninsula
British Columbia

Life Span: 20 years or more

Current Status: Near Threatened (IUCN)

EXTINCT

EXTINCT IN THE WILD

CRITICALLY ENDANGERED

ENDANGERED

VULNERABLE

NEAR THREATENED

LEAST CONCERN

Researchers still have much to learn about the blue shark. They rely on the support of governments and individuals to help protect the species. Today, a few countries limit the number of blue sharks that can be caught each year. The United States and other countries have banned blue shark finning.

Certain fishing practices keep blue sharks safe. Many people use special hooks that are less likely to catch a blue shark. Some fishing nets allow sharks to break free. With the help of people all over the world, the blue shark is on track to survive long into the future.

GLOSSARY

ampullae of Lorenzini—a network of tiny jelly-filled sacs around a shark's snout; the jelly is sensitive to the electric fields of nearby prey.

bycatch—animals that are accidentally caught with fishing nets or lines

cartilage—firm, flexible connective tissue that makes up a shark's skeleton

countershading—coloring that helps camouflage an animal; fish with countershading have pale bellies and dark backs.

dermal denticles—small, tooth-like scales that cover some types of fish

dorsal fins—the fins on the back of a fish

ecosystem—a community of organisms and their environment

electric fields—waves of electricity created by movement; every living being has an electric field.

finning—the practice of cutting off a shark's fins at sea and tossing the shark back into the water

gill rakers—thousands of fine bristles in the blue shark's throat; gill rakers strain krill, anchovies, and other tiny creatures from water.

lateral lines—a system of tubes beneath a shark's skin that helps it detect changes in water pressure

mature—to become old enough to reproduce; blue sharks mature between 4 and 6 years old.

migrate—to move from one place to another, often with the seasons

near threatened—could soon be at risk of becoming endangered

nictitating membranes—whitish inner eyelids that close to protect a shark's eyes when it attacks prey

pectoral fins—a pair of fins that extend from each side of a fish's body

serrated—having a jagged edge

viviparous—producing young that develop inside the body; viviparous animals give birth to live young.

TO LEARN MORE

At the Library

Berman, Ruth. *Sharks*. Minneapolis, Minn.: Lerner Publications, 2009.

Kalman, Bobbie, and Molly Aloian. *Spectacular Sharks*. New York, N.Y.: Crabtree Pub. Co., 2003.

Wilsdon, Christina. *Sharks*. Pleasantville, N.Y.: Reader's Digest Young Families, 2007.

On the Web

Learning more about blue sharks is as easy as 1, 2, 3.

1. Go to www.factsurfer.com.

2. Enter "blue sharks" into the search box.

3. Click the "Surf" button and you will see a list of related Web sites.

With factsurfer.com, finding more information is just a click away.

INDEX